B55 074 054 0

STRANGE BEASTS

by Nel Yomtov

raintree
a Capstone company — publishers for children

Raintree is an imprint of Capstone Global Library Limited, a company incorporated in England and Wales having its registered office at 264 Banbury Road, Oxford, OX2 7DY – Registered company number: 6695582

www.raintree.co.uk
myorders@raintree.co.uk

Edited by Mandy Robbins
Designed by Kyle Grenz
Original illustrations © Capstone Global Library Limited 2021
Picture research by Kelly Garvin
Production by Kathy McColley
Originated by Capstone Global Library Ltd
Printed and bound in India

978 1 3982 0436 2 (hardback)
978 1 3982 0437 9 (paperback)

British Library Cataloguing in Publication Data
A full catalogue record for this book is available from the British Library.

Acknowledgements
We would like to thank the following for permission to reproduce photographs: Alamy: Michael Patrick O'Neill, 43, Papilio, 31, Solvin Zankl, 38; Minden Pictures: David Shale, 37, Murray Cooper, 25; Newscom: Alessandra Sarti imageBROKER, 34, Kerryn Parkinson/ NORFANZ, 41, Morten Strange/ NHPA/Photoshot, 23; Science Source : Danté Fenolio, 39, Nicholas Smythe, 13; Shutterstock: Ann Kolesnikova, 40, Anna Veselova, 17, argus, (sparks) design element throughout, Artush, 14, Butterfly Hunter, 19, chempina, (fish) Cover, Chris Watson, 32, Dan Olsen, 4, Dennis van de Water, 30, Dr Morley Read, bottom 5, feathercollector, 21, G.J. Verspui, 27, 29, Gaulois_s, bottom 33, Hein Nouwens, 1, Hussein Shaharuddin, left Cover, Kurit afshen, 26, Lisa Stelzel, 45, Manu M Nair, right Cover, Marc Witte, 35, mark higgins, top 33, Martin Mecnarowski, 10, Neil Bromhall, 7, 8, 9, RudiErnst, 11, vadimmmus, top 5, Verpeya, 15

CONTENTS

Words in **bold** are in the glossary.

A curious collection of bizarre beasts

If you think your pets behave weirdly, you haven't seen anything yet! Scientists have discovered up to 1.3 million **species** of animals. Among them are thousands of weird creatures that look and behave like nothing you've ever seen before. Some animals have enormous, bulging eyes, such as the aye-aye. The thorny devil has horns on its skin. Most of all animal life on Earth is actually insects. One example is the giraffe-necked weevil, with its long, odd-looking neck. A further look at the animal kingdom reveals purple squirrels, flying mammals and see-through frogs. All of these strange beasts are completely captivating.

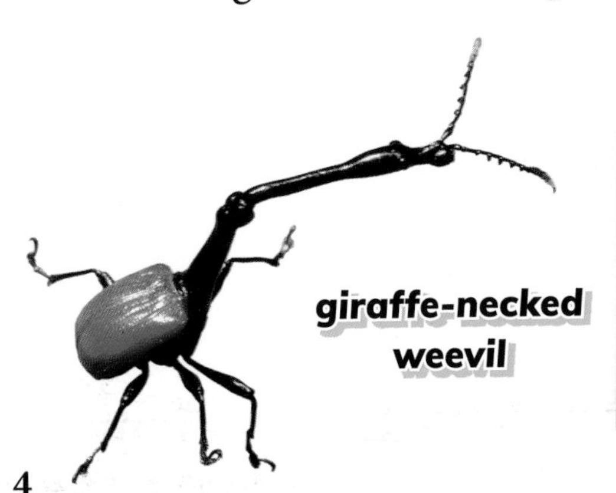
giraffe-necked weevil

Fact!

In 2018, scientists at the Natural History Museum in London discovered 272 more species of animals.

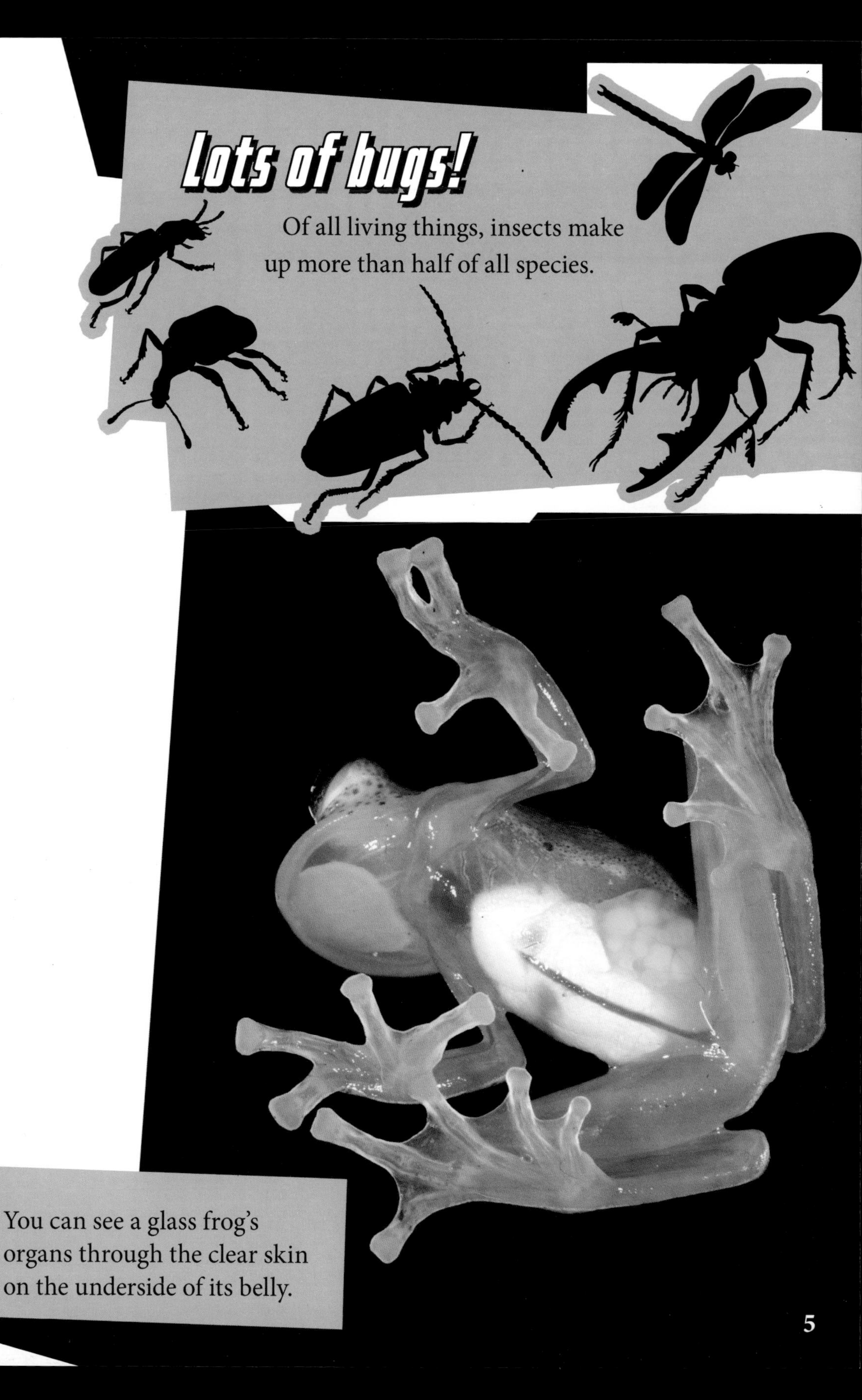

Lots of bugs!

Of all living things, insects make up more than half of all species.

You can see a glass frog's organs through the clear skin on the underside of its belly.

Mysterious mammals

Naked mole rat

Naked mole rats are found in eastern Africa, especially in the countries of Ethiopia, Somalia and Kenya. Some people say they look like tiny walruses. These weird and wrinkly **rodents** have a hairless, tube-like body with pink or greyish-pink skin. Because they have very tiny eyes, mole rats are nearly blind.

Breathing easy

There is very little air to breathe underground. But naked mole rats have **adapted** to the airless conditions. They have small lungs, and their blood is very good at carrying oxygen throughout their bodies. In one study, mole rats were able to survive 18 minutes without air! In comparison, the human brain can be damaged after only 3 minutes without air.

A naked mole rat holds its food in its front paws while eating.

Naked mole rats are usually about 7.5 centimetres (3 in) long. They weigh around 43 grams (1.5 oz). The queen is the largest member of a mole rat **colony**. She can weigh up to 71 grams (2.5 oz).

These tiny creatures are digging machines. Using their powerful jaws and snouts, they dig long tunnels and nests underground. Tunnel systems can measure up to 4 kilometres (2.5 mi) long and contain up to 300 mole rats. One queen controls the entire colony.

The naked mole rat doesn't just look weird. It also has strange eating habits. Naked mole rats eat the underground parts of plants, such as roots and bulbs. They usually leave enough of the plant for it to keep growing. Then it can be another meal. Naked mole rats also eat their own poo! It has special **nutrients** the mole rats can use. They are also among the few animal species that do not drink water. Mole rats get all the water they need from the plants they eat.

A naked mole rat eats the roots that hang down in its underground tunnel.

Fact!

The four large front teeth of the naked mole rat sit outside the mouth. This position keeps the animal from eating dirt when digging.

A naked mole rat peeks out of its tunnel.

Naked mole rats have amazing health compared to other rodents. They show few signs of ageing. Naked mole rats rarely get cancer. They can live longer than 30 years. But most live less than a year or two because so many **predators** hunt them.

An Indian giant squirrel munches on a bunch of berries.

Indian giant squirrel

The world's most colourful rodent, the Indian giant squirrel, is found in eastern and southern India. Many people call this furry creature the "Rainbow Squirrel". Its brilliant colours range from deep red to purple, cream to light brown and bright orange to deep brown.

The Indian giant squirrel is much bigger than other squirrels. It measures about 1 metre (3 ft) from head to tail. That's twice the size of common grey squirrels. The Indian giant squirrel can also leap more than 6 metres (20 ft). It jumps between tree limbs in forests.

The squirrel's diet includes fruit, nuts, tree bark, flowers, insects and bird eggs. Other squirrels store their food underground. But Indian giant squirrels store their food in nests they build in treetops. Their patchy, dark colours blend in with the colours of leaves, tree branches and flowers. They help the squirrel hide from its main predators, leopards and serpent eagles.

An Indian giant squirrel clings to a tree branch between jumps.

Pink fairy armadillo

The pink fairy armadillo is the world's smallest armadillo. It is just 13 centimetres (5 in) long. This little creature is found in the dry grasslands and sandy plains in central Argentina. It spends its time digging through the earth and feeding on plants, ants and worms. Its hard shell is made up of 24 bands of armour to protect its back and head. Fur under the armour keeps the body warm.

Room to breathe

The pink fairy armadillo has a hard butt plate at its back end. As the animal digs with its claws, it pushes the soil under its body towards its rear. The butt plate pats down the soil and pushes it back. The animal slides back slightly as it does this, leaving an empty space in front to breathe.

The pink fairy armadillo is tiny and almost impossible to find. Because it spends most of its life burrowing underground, it is rarely seen. Scientist Mariella Superina studied the creature's habitat in South America for 13 years. In all that time, she never saw one in the wild! Pink fairy armadillos can't survive outside their natural surroundings, so they are very difficult to study. For this reason, not much is known about their behaviour.

Pink fairy armadillos have large front claws for digging.

Aye-aye

The aye-aye is a lemur. This type of **primate** is related to chimpanzees, apes and humans. It is found only on Madagascar, a large island off the east coast of Africa. Its odd appearance and odd eating habits make the aye-aye one of the world's strangest primates.

Aye-ayes are dark brown or black. They have a large bushy tail, huge round eyes, thin fingers and large, moveable ears.

An aye-aye scans the forest floor from high up in the trees.

Aye-ayes are the largest type of primate that are active only at night. An average male is about 35 to 43 centimetres (14 to 17 in) long, not including its tail. It weighs 2 kilograms (4 lbs). Females are slightly smaller and weigh less. Aye-ayes live in rainforests and swamps. They move quickly and can travel down tree trunks either head first or tail first. They build their nests at the tops of tall trees. The nests are oval shaped with a single entry hole.

Animal life on Madagascar

The island of Madagascar is home to hundreds of different animal species. Many species are found nowhere else in the world.

Type	Number of species (estimated)
mammals	100
amphibians	300
reptiles	350
birds	280

The aye-aye's weirdest physical feature helps it hunt. On each hand, it has an extra-long, crooked middle finger. The finger can swivel in any direction! At night, the aye-aye prowls along tree branches tapping the finger on tree bark. It shifts its ears forward and listens carefully to any sounds made by **prey** living inside the branches. They are usually grubs or **larvae**. It also listens to echoes from the tapping of its finger. The echoes sound different when insects are there. This process is called **echolocation**.

If the aye-aye hears food in the branch, it chews a hole in the bark with its long, sharp teeth. Then it works its flexible middle finger into the hole and digs out dinner.

Fact!

The only other animal known to hunt for food by tapping is the woodpecker.

An aye-aye taps on a tree trunk with its long middle finger to search for food.

Echolocation

Echolocation is a method some animals use to locate objects. The animal makes a sound and then listens for its sound waves to bounce off another object.

The aye-aye taps on tree branches to make a sound. If there are bugs inside the branches, the echo coming back makes a special sound. Aye-ayes can tap up to eight times a second. They spend nearly half their time tapping to find prey.

Funky fliers

Colugo

Look up! It's not a bird. It's not a plane. It's a colugo! This adorable mammal may look like it's flying, but it's actually gliding. Colugos are called flying lemurs. A colugo looks like a combination of a small squirrel and a bat. Colugos are found in the tropical forests of Southeast Asia. Adult colugos measure up to 40 centimetres (16 in) and weigh as much as 2 kilograms (4.5 lbs). Only two species of colugos exist in the world.

This small, furry animal is perfectly adapted for gliding. A large, fur-covered **membrane** of skin stretches from its face to the tips of its webbed feet and tail. This giant flap of skin lets it glide more than 60 metres (200 ft) from tree to tree. Its webbed feet also help it glide, and its strong, needle-sharp claws help it grip tree trunks and branches.

A colugo uses its sharp claws to hold on to a tree trunk.

Adapting to forest life

The colugo's membrane is only one of several adaptations that help the creature survive in its environment. The soles of its feet can form suction cups that help it land and grab things. The colugo also has a set of tiny lower teeth that looks like a comb. Scientists believe the comb-like structure helps the animal feed and clean itself.

Rhinoceros hornbill

If you've ever had a noisy neighbour, you'll know what it's like to live next to the rhinoceros hornbill. This large bird is found in parts of Southeast Asia. It grows up to 127 centimetres (50 inches) long and weighs as much as 2.9 kilograms (6.5 lb).

The rhinoceros hornbill is a black and white bird. It has a spectacular horn on the top of its head called a casque. This horn is made of the same material that makes up human fingernails. It is hollow inside. The casque helps to turn up the volume of the bird's loud, echoing calls over long distances. The calls communicate with other hornbills to warn of danger or to simply make the bird's presence known.

The colour of the casque is creamy white when the bird is born. Over time, the bird makes its bill a brilliant orange colour. It does this by rubbing the bill against a gland beneath its tail that contains an orange-red oil. It takes six years for the casque to fully develop its striking look.

A pair of rhinoceros hornbills perch on a tree branch in Indonesia.

The rhinoceros hornbill has one of nature's most unusual child-raising techniques. When the female is ready to lay her eggs, she works with the male to find a narrow crack in a hollowed-out tree. They build a nest there. The couple works together to close the female inside with mud, fruit and their own poo. They leave a small hole. The male guards the nest. He uses his long beak to pass food to the female and the babies through the hole. The female empties her nest of poo through the same hole.

A month after the chicks are born, the female breaks out! Then both parents reseal the hole. For the next two months, the mother and father hunt for food and deliver it to the growing chicks. When the chicks have their feathers, the parents open the hole and release the babies from the nest.

Fact!

Rhinoceros hornbills mate for life.

A male rhinoceros hornbill guards his family nest.

Long-wattled umbrellabird

The long-wattled umbrellabird lives in the rainforests and lowlands of western Colombia and Ecuador. The all-black male has a tuft of feathers that hangs over its bill. It looks a bit like an umbrella. The bird's most unique feature is the long **wattle** that hangs from its throat to the middle of the chest.

The male umbrellabird throws an all-out dance party when it's time to find a mate. These dances are called leks. To attract a female, the male inflates his wattle and swings it back and forth. This makes his mating call louder and displays his wattle's full splendour. The male makes loud grunts and booming sounds. They can be heard more than 975 metres (3,200 ft) away.

A male long-wattled umbrellabird displays his impressive wattle.

Fact!

The cutting down of trees and hunting threatens to destroy the umbrellabird's natural environment.

Creepy creatures

Glass frog

You don't have to be a scientist to see how the glass frog got its name. This tiny frog has see-through skin on its belly and chest. You can see its beating heart, blood vessels, bones, liver, intestines and more. The top side of the frog is usually coloured green to blend in with its environment. Glass frogs measure 2.5 to 7.6 centimetres (1 to 3 in) long.

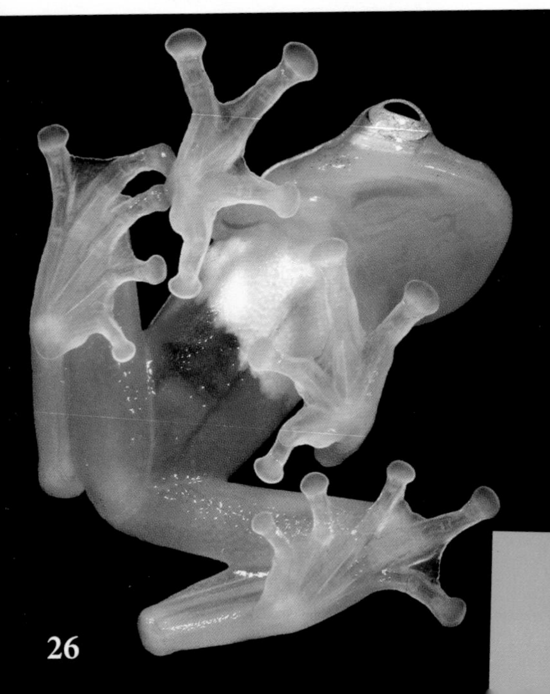

Only the underside of the glass frog's body has see-through skin.

From the front and the top, a glass frog looks green, like most other frogs.

About 150 species of glass frogs live in the rainforests of Central and South America. They hunt at night, looking for insects and spiders to eat. The eyes of the tree frog are adapted to see better in the dark. They are large and bright. Unlike most other frogs whose eyes face to the sides, the eyes of the glass frog face straight ahead. This helps them find prey.

As parents, glass frogs aren't your ordinary neighbourhood croakers. Most frogs lay their eggs in small bodies of water. The female glass frog lays her eggs on the underside of leaves high above streams or ponds. She sticks them in place with a gooey liquid. Then she leaves and returns to the treetops.

The male guards the eggs until they hatch. He protects them from enemies such as wasps and snakes.

When the eggs hatch, the tiny **tadpoles** drop into the water below. They live there for about a year, growing legs and losing their tails. Then they crawl out of the water to live among the trees and plants.

Fact!

In 2017, scientists discovered a new species of glass frog in Ecuador. The tiny creature was about 2 centimetres (0.8 in) long!

A male glass frog guards his eggs.

Glass frogs are extremely delicate. Because of this, they have to hide when it rains hard. A glass frog can be washed off a leaf by heavy rainfall. Some have been killed from a direct hit by a single drop of rain.

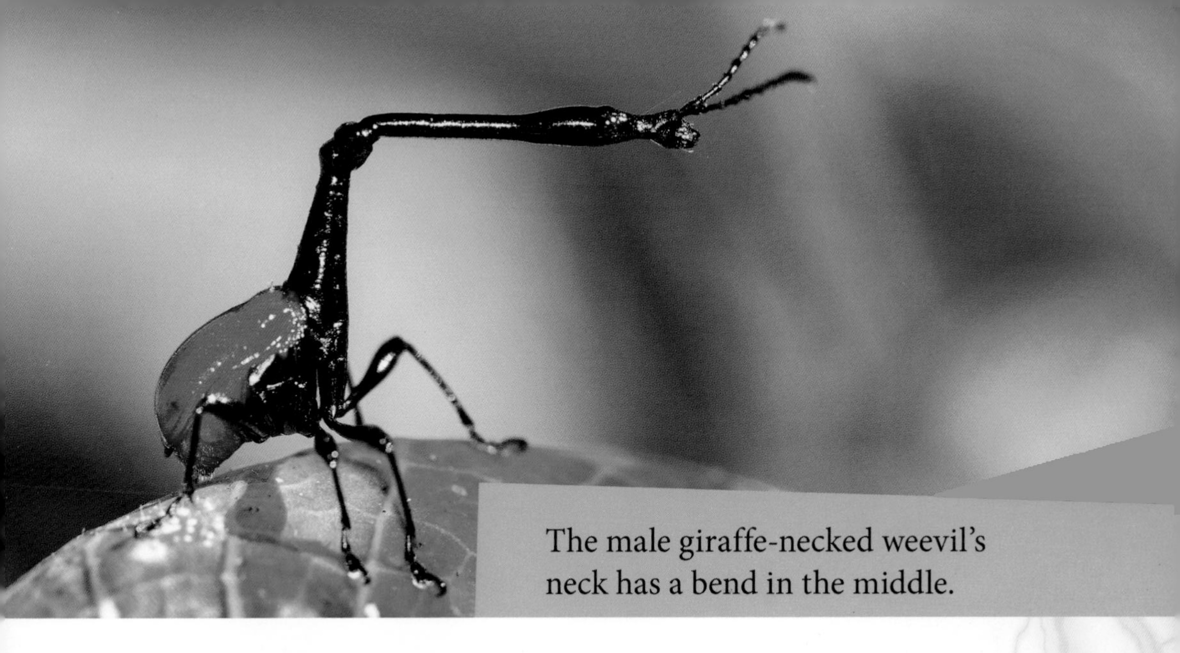

The male giraffe-necked weevil's neck has a bend in the middle.

Giraffe-necked weevil

It's easy to guess how the giraffe-necked weevil got its name! This bizarre bug grows to about 2.5 centimetres (1 in). Its body is black with an orange or red shell that covers the back. The shell protects the weevil's back wings. The insect also has a long neck like a giraffe. The male has a much longer neck than the female. Weevils live their entire lives in trees and feed on leaves.

Giraffe-necked weevils are the warriors of the insect world. During the mating season, males compete for females by pushing and wrestling each other with their long necks. The winner mates with the female.

After mating, the female lays an egg. She places it on a leaf. She rolls up the leaf with her long neck and snips the leaf so that it falls to the forest floor with the egg inside. When the egg hatches, the larva feeds on the leaf it was wrapped in.

The female giraffe-necked weevil (left) has a much shorter neck than the male (right).

Fact!

Though they're known as fighters, giraffe-necked weevils are rarely deadly. They don't harm other species. Even during mating combat, the males rarely kill each other.

Thorny devil

The country of Australia is home to some of Earth's most unusual wildlife. One of these is the thorny devil. This horned lizard is quite incredible looking. Its head and the top of its body are covered in spikes and scales. These features help the lizard defend itself against enemies. The thorny devil also sports a false head on the back of its neck. Adults reach a length of 20 centimetres (8 in) and weigh up to 96 grams (3.4 oz). Despite their relatively small size, these hardy creatures can live for up to 20 years in the wild. As desert dwellers, their diet is ants, ants and more ants! In a single meal, a thorny devil can eat more than 3,000 ants.

The thorny devil's colours blend in well with the Australian wilderness where it lives.

thorny devil

Australian folklore

The thorny devil plays an important role in stories of Australia's native people. According to legend, the lizard carried brown and yellow colours in a pouch it wore around its neck. The thorny devil placed the colours throughout the land. This is how the Australian desert got its colours. For centuries, Aboriginal people have used these same colours to decorate their bodies.

The lizard's false head comes in handy when the creature goes into survival mode. When threatened, it tucks its real head down between its legs for protection. The false head remains where the real head once was. To further discourage hungry predators, the thorny devil puffs up its chest to appear larger. This scares off enemies and make the lizard harder to eat.

A thorny devil tucks its head down, displaying its false head.

A thorny devil's spikes and spines vary in size.

The thorny devil is well-suited to living in the harsh, dry desert. It has tiny, moisture-attracting grooves between its spikes and scales. During the night, dew collects in these grooves. The tiny grooves guide the water to the lizard's mouth. Thorny devils can also absorb moisture by burying themselves into wet sand after it rains. This process allows the creature to take in water from any part of its body.

Dwellers of the seas

Deep-sea anglerfish

The deep-sea anglerfish looks like something out of a nightmare! This fish has a narrow body, huge head, gaping mouth and pointed teeth. But its most unusual feature is a flexible rod that sticks out above its mouth like a fishing pole. Only females have this rod. The tip of the rod glows to attract prey, such as worms, shellfish or other fish. When the prey approaches, the anglerfish snatches it up in its huge mouth.

Deep-sea anglerfish are most commonly found in the waters off the coast of Europe in the Atlantic Ocean. They live in waters as deep as 2,010 metres (6,600 feet) below the surface.

Fact!

Tiny bacteria produce the light at the end of the female anglerfish's rod. The light is also used to attract a mate.

Within the animal kingdom, females are often larger than males. Compared to female anglerfish, males are positively puny. The largest females reach about 76 centimetres (2.5 ft) long. The smallest males of the species are less than 1.3 centimetres (0.5 in) long.

A female deep-sea anglerfish waits for prey with her mouth open.

The deep-sea anglerfish has a bizarre way of reproducing. The male uses its sharp, hook-like teeth to attach to the female's body. He bites into her skin and releases a chemical that joins his mouth to her body. The two travel together as one. The male gets all of his nutrition from the female's blood. When the female is ready to release her eggs, the male is right there to fertilize them. Then, the male detaches itself.

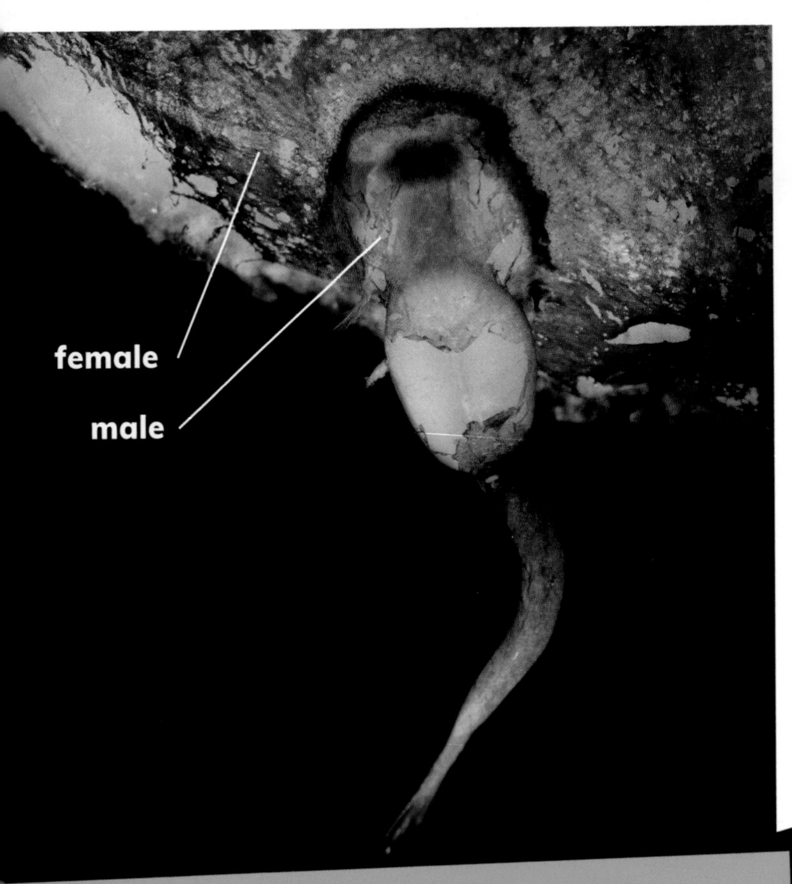

The much smaller male deep-sea anglerfish attaches to a female.

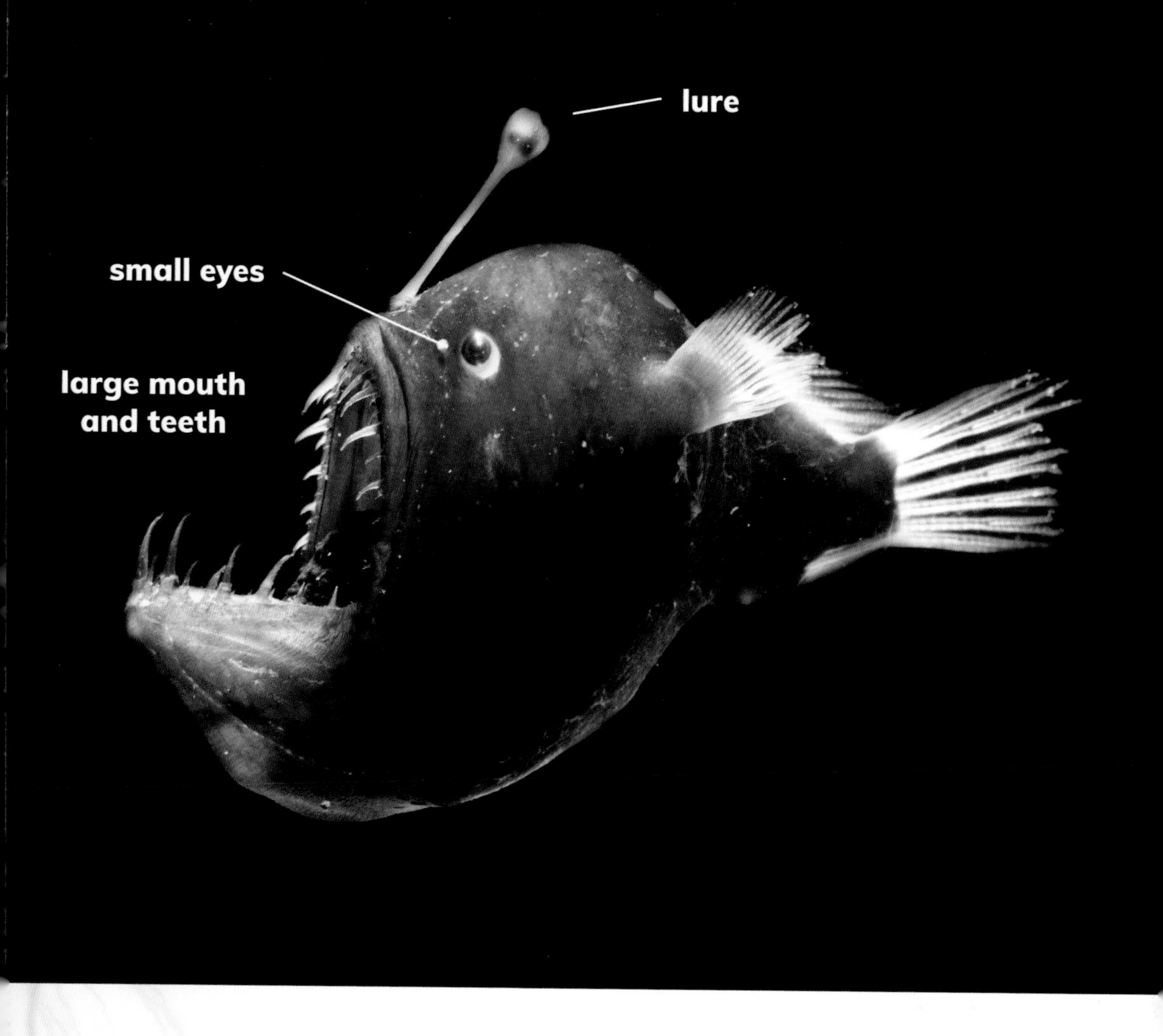

Scientists first identified anglerfish in 1833, when a female was found off the coast of Greenland. Since then, about 170 species of anglerfish have been recorded. One anglerfish found off West Africa had its glowing lure located inside its huge mouth!

Blobfish

In 2013, the Ugly Animal Preservation Society voted the blobfish as the ugliest animal on Earth. This droopy creature lives off the coast of Australia at depths of more than 610 metres (2,000 ft). The water pressure there is 120 times greater than at the surface. At such depths, the pressure would easily crush a human body.

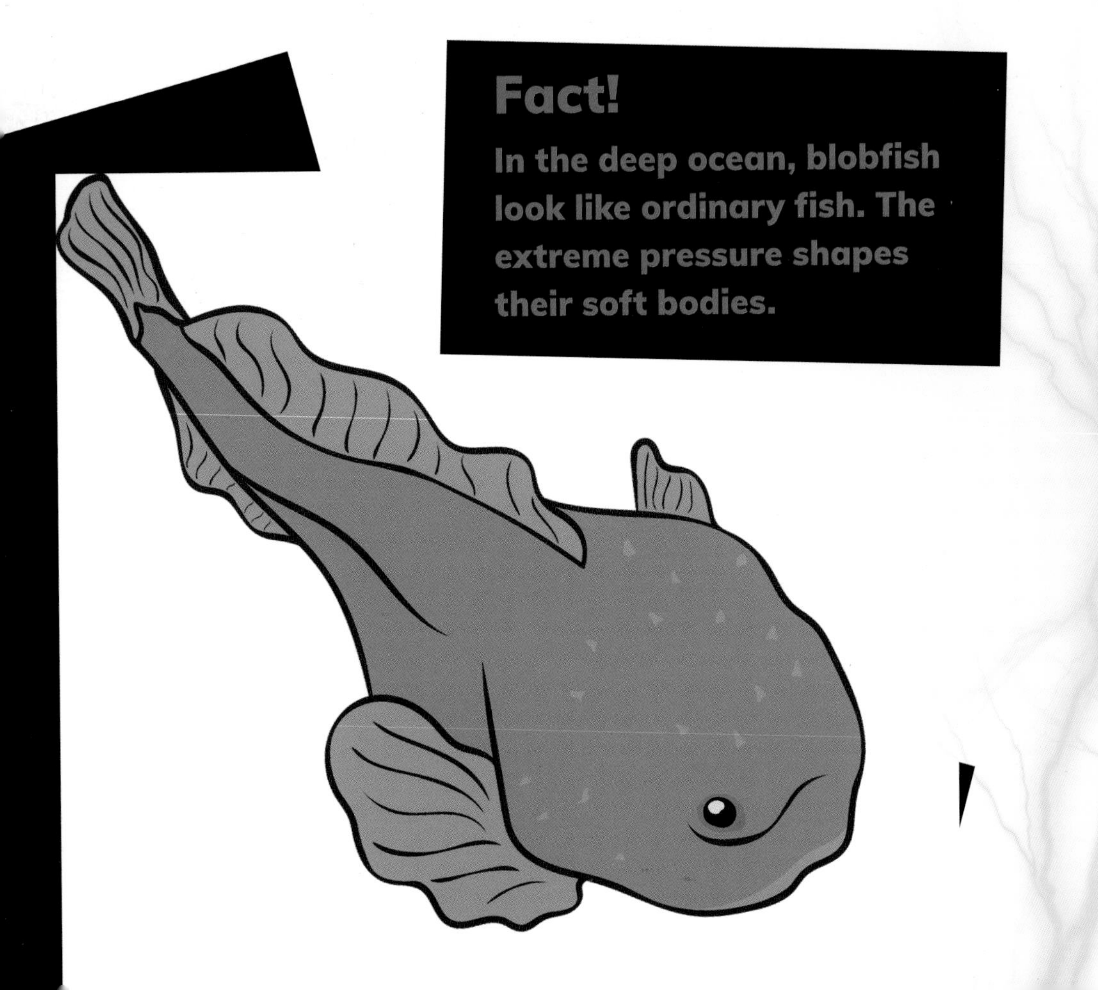

Fact!

In the deep ocean, blobfish look like ordinary fish. The extreme pressure shapes their soft bodies.

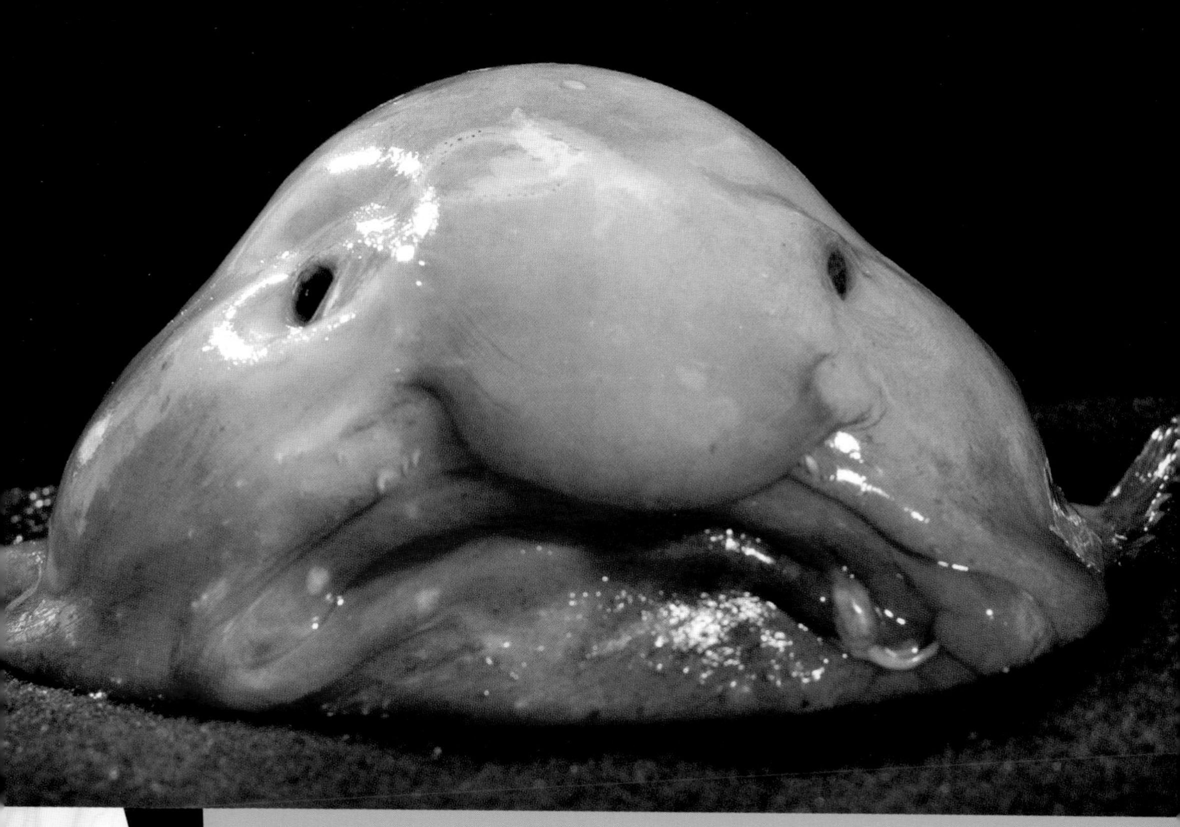

When scientists or fishermen drag blobfish to the surface, they "blob" out because there is no pressure to maintain their shape.

The blobfish has adapted to live in this harsh environment. The fish is made of jelly-like flesh. Its bones are very soft, and it has very little muscle. Unlike most fish, the blobfish does not have an air sac. This gas-filled sac helps other fish swim through the water without sinking. The blobfish has no air sac because it would collapse under high pressure. Rather than swim, the blobfish simply floats just above the seafloor.

Northern stargazer

Its name sounds dreamlike, but don't let that fool you. The northern stargazer is one of the most fearsome fish you'll ever see. It lives in the waters along the eastern coast of the United States. If looks could kill, this beast would win first prize. The stargazer earns its name for the position of its eyes. They're on top of its head, always looking up.

The stargazer's hunting methods are rather shocking – literally. It uses its side fins to shovel away sand and buries itself in the ocean floor. With its eyes and mouth barely sticking out of the sand, it patiently waits for prey to approach. When food passes by, the stargazer zaps it with electricity. This zap is delivered from organs located behind the fish's eyes! The dazed prey then floats helplessly into the stargazer's mouth.

Fact!

The northern stargazer can grow to 56 centimetres (22 in) long and weigh about 9 kilograms (20 lbs).

A northern stargazer hides on the ocean floor waiting to zap prey.

BUT WAIT ...
THERE'S MORE

Goblin shark

The goblin shark lives in the deep, dark seas where there is little light. The creature's most distinctive features are its long snout and extending jaw. The snout has special organs to sense the electric fields created by other fish. This helps it locate prey in the low light. When the shark senses food, it closes in and thrusts out its jaw to snag the prey!

Red-lipped batfish

The red-lipped batfish lives off the western coast of Ecuador in South America. It looks like it's wearing bright red lipstick. If that weren't odd enough, it uses its fins like legs. This fish walks on the ocean floor.

The stinky hoatzin bird rests on a branch in the Amazon Rainforest.

Hoatzin

Hoatzins are plant-eating birds. When they process food, their body makes awful-smelling chemicals that the bird then burps out. For this reason, hoatzins are also called stink birds or skunk birds.

Panda ant

The panda ant isn't actually an ant at all. It's a wasp. It is found in Chile. The sting of the panda ant is so painful, it's also called the cow-killer ant.

GLOSSARY

adapt change in order to survive

colony group of animals living together

echolocation process of using sounds and echoes to locate objects

larva insect at the stage of development between an egg and an adult

membrane thin, flexible layers of skin

nutrient substance needed by a living thing to stay healthy

predator animal that hunts another animal for food

prey animal hunted by another for food

primate any animal in the group of mammals that includes humans, apes and monkeys

rodent mammal with long front teeth used for gnawing

species animals with similar features

tadpole stage of a frog between the egg and adult stages

wattle piece of skin that hangs down from the chin of some birds

FIND OUT MORE

BOOKS

Amazing Animals: More than 100 of the World's Most Remarkable Creatures, Claire Hibbert (Arcturus, 2021)

Animal Adaptations (On Topic), Ruth Bjorklund (Raintree, 2020)

Knowledge Encyclopedia Animal!, John Woodward (DK Children, 2016)

WEBSITES

www.bbc.co.uk/bitesize/topics/zvhhvcw/articles/zxg7y4j
Learn more about how animals adapt to their environments at BBC Bitesize.

www.dkfindout.com/uk/animals-and-nature
Learn more about animals with DKfindout!.

www.natgeokids.com/uk/category/discover/animals/
Discover more about all kinds of animals with National Geographic.

INDEX